A TRUE BOOK

Tornadoes

STEVEN OTFINOSKI

Children's Press®
An Imprint of Scholastic Inc.

SO-AJE-476

Content Consultant
William Barnart, PhD
Assistant Professor
Department of Earth and Environmental Sciences
University of Iowa
Iowa City, Iowa

Library of Congress Cataloging-in-Publication Data
Otfinoski, Steven, author.
Tornadoes / by Steven Otfinoski.
   pages cm. — (A true book)
 Summary: "Learn all about tornadoes, from what causes them to what effects they have on
humans."— Provided by publisher.
 Includes bibliographical references and index.
 ISBN 978-0-531-22297-3 (library binding) — ISBN 978-0-531-22513-4 (pbk.)
 1. Tornadoes—Juvenile literature. I. Title. II. Series: True book.
 QC955.2.O84 2016
 551.55'3—dc23   2015025187

No part of this publication may be reproduced in whole or in part, or stored in a retrieval system,
or transmitted in any form or by any means, electronic, mechanical, photocopying, recording, or
otherwise, without written permission of the publisher. For information regarding permission,
write to Scholastic Inc., Attention: Permissions Department, 557 Broadway, New York, NY 10012.

© 2016 Scholastic Inc.
All rights reserved. Published in 2016 by Children's Press, an imprint of Scholastic Inc.
Printed in China 62
SCHOLASTIC, CHILDREN'S PRESS, A TRUE BOOK™, and associated logos are trademarks and/or
registered trademarks of Scholastic Inc.
1 2 3 4 5 6 7 8 9 10 R 25 24 23 22 21 20 19 18 17 16

**Front cover: Professional storm chasers
monitor an approaching tornado
Back cover: Houses destroyed by a tornado**

Find the Truth!

Everything you are about to read is true *except* for one of the sentences on this page.

Which one is **TRUE**?

T or F More tornadoes happen in the United States than anywhere else on Earth.

T or F Only hurricanes have faster, more powerful winds than tornadoes.

Find the answers in this book.

Contents

THE BIG TRUTH!

Storm Chasers

Students practice a tornado drill.

4 Means of Survival

How can you survive a tornado?

5 Tracking Tornadoes

How are experts collecting data to better understand tornadoes?

Weather radar stations sometimes detect birds, planes, or even insect swarms.

A tornado moves
through Xenia, Ohio,
on April 3, 1974.

Disaster in Xenia

Eighteen-year-old Ruth Venuti was waiting for a ride home from school when she saw a black cloud in the sky. It was huge, swirling, and headed straight for Xenia High School. It didn't take Venuti long to realize that it was a tornado. It was 4:25 PM, and the only people left in the school were a group of students rehearsing a play with their teacher David Heath. Venuti rushed into the building to warn them.

Three of every four tornadoes in the world occur in the United States.

Just in Time

Heath thought Venuti was joking. Then he went outside and saw for himself that there really was a tornado bearing down on the school. With only moments to spare, Heath herded the students into the school's central hallway. They pressed their bodies against the walls as rushing winds crashed through the windows. Broken glass, wood, and mud swept past them. The wind's roar was deafening.

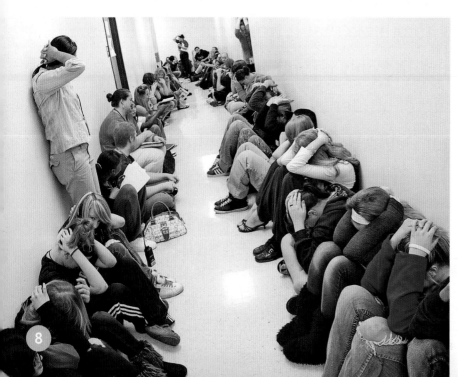

In areas where tornadoes are likely to occur, students and teachers routinely participate in drills to practice what they will do in case of a real tornado.

Another tornado struck Xenia on September 20, 2000, killing one man and damaging more than 300 homes and 30 businesses.

A School Destroyed

The chaos was over in four minutes. "There was total silence," Heath later recalled. Incredibly, no one was seriously injured. However, the school was destroyed. The entire top floor was ripped off. On the stage where the students had been rehearsing only minutes before lay an overturned school bus. The tornado had picked it up and dropped it there.

Xenia residents sort through the wreckage of a home after the 1974 tornado.

A Town Devastated

Other Xenia residents were not as fortunate as the students. The tornado killed 33 people and injured more than 1,300 others. Some 1,400 buildings, including 1,200 homes, were destroyed or damaged. The tornado picked up a tractor-trailer truck and dropped it onto the roof of a bowling alley. It was one of the worst tornado disasters ever to hit American soil.

The Super Outbreak

The tornado that hit Xenia that day was just one of 148 that struck dozens of communities on April 3 and 4, 1974 (pictured). In just 16 hours, tornadoes touched ground in 13 states and Ontario, Canada. This "Super **Outbreak**" claimed a total of 335 lives and injured more than 6,000 people. Property damage totaled $600 million. It remains the second-worst tornado outbreak in U.S. history. The worst occurred in April 2011 and stretched across the Southeastern and Midwestern United States. In that outbreak, some 350 tornadoes touched down, killing 316 people.

Stamping Ground, Kentucky, was one of the many towns affected by the Super Outbreak.

In the Northern Hemisphere, most tornadoes spin cyclonically, or in a counterclockwise direction. In the Southern Hemisphere, they spin clockwise.

CHAPTER 2

Funnels of Fury

Twisters. Cyclones. Tornadoes. Whatever name you choose to call them, these storms pack a powerful punch. Hurricanes usually reach full strength at around 75 miles per hour (121 kilometers per hour). Tornadoes have been recorded at more than four times that speed. With such powerful winds, tornadoes can lift cars into the air, hurl people to their deaths, and flatten entire towns. No storms on Earth are more destructive.

What Is a Tornado?

A tornado is a powerful, twisting storm that forms out of thunderstorms. Because its winds spin, it is often called a twister. In the United States, thunderstorms arise when cool, dry air from Canada meets up with warm, humid air from the Gulf of Mexico. The most violent thunderstorms that produce heavy rains and hailstones are called **supercells**. They are the most likely to give birth to tornadoes.

A thunderstorm's strong rains and wind can give way to even more dangerous conditions under the right circumstances.

Tornadoes are formed because of a meeting of hot and cold air.

The color of a tornado is determined by the **debris** it carries.

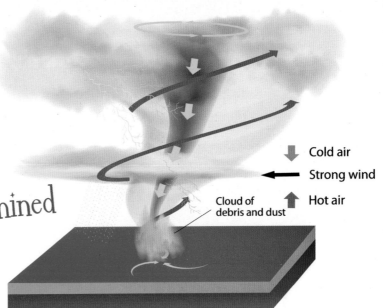

Cold air

Strong wind

Hot air

Cloud of debris and dust

The Life of a Twister

As a thunderstorm grows in intensity, masses of warm air rise swiftly and are continually replaced by more warm air masses. As the air rises, it starts to rotate. This circulation of air forms a funnel called a **vortex**. The vortex stretches down from the storm clouds to form a long, thin column. Only when the column touches the ground does it become a tornado. The tornado picks up and carries anything in its path— dirt, trees, rocks, and even broken bits of buildings.

Most tornadoes strike between the hours of 4:00 and 9:00 PM.

A tornado can level an entire town in minutes.

Small, Short-Lived, and Destructive

Most tornadoes die in a short time because they quickly run out of the moist, warm air that drives them. The average tornado lasts only three minutes and travels a distance of 6 miles (10 km). Tornadoes lasting longer than 15 minutes are rare. Compared to hurricanes and other storms, tornadoes cover a very small area. Most of them measure just a few hundred yards or meters in **diameter**. But even in a few minutes, the concentrated power of a tornado can be extremely destructive.

Where and When

Tornadoes occur on every continent except Antarctica. However, most tornadoes—about 1,200 a year—take place in the United States. Most of these occur in the Great Plains of the Midwest and the Southeast. This area is called Tornado Alley. Other places where tornadoes are common are northern Europe, western Asia, Japan, Australia, and New Zealand. Most tornadoes in the United States occur in spring and early summer, when the masses of warm and cold air most frequently meet.

Great Plains states such as Kansas are among the most likely places for a tornado to touch down.

Measuring Tornadoes

Tornadoes are measured in part by the destruction they leave behind. **Meteorologist** Ted Fujita, known as "Mr. Tornado," devised his Fujita Scale for tornadoes in 1988. It was revised in 2007. The Enhanced Fujita (EF) Scale rates tornadoes in six categories. EF0 denotes a tornado of 65 to 85 miles per hour (105 to 137 kph) that causes light damage to roofs and trees. At the other end of the spectrum is an EF5 tornado, which reaches speeds of more than 200 miles per hour (322 kph) and causes massive destruction.

Ted Fujita studies a simulated tornado at his Chicago laboratory in 1979.

Additional vortexes can greatly increase a tornado's ability to cause damage.

A series of eight tornadoes traveled 294 miles (473 km) through Illinois and Indiana in 1917.

Outbreaks and Multi-Vortexes

Sometimes large supercells can produce a whole family of tornadoes. All these tornadoes may appear at once along the path of a single thunderstorm. Other times, one tornado will trigger the next, creating a series of twisters. In a tornado outbreak like the one that took place in April 1974, dozens of tornadoes can develop out of a widespread storm. Occasionally, a single tornado can grow multiple funnels or vortexes.

Most tornadoes occur in places where there are few people or buildings.

CHAPTER 3

Legendary Twisters

The majority of tornadoes are small and fairly weak. They appear in remote areas where they do little harm. However, those few powerful twisters that strike where there are homes and businesses can do incredible damage. The worst of them can devastate entire communities. Read on to learn about some of the most destructive twisters in history.

Only about 20 percent of all supercell thunderstorms produce tornadoes.

The town of Natchez, Mississippi, was the namesake of the devastating 1840 tornado.

The Great Natchez Tornado

Before the 20th century, people had few safeguards and little warning when tornadoes struck. They found themselves completely at nature's mercy. Such was the case on May 7, 1840, when a huge tornado tore along the Mississippi River. Along its 20-mile (32 km) path, it claimed 317 lives and injured an additional 109 people. Large boats on the river were swallowed up by the storm. It is the only American tornado on record where deaths outnumbered injuries.

The Tri-State Tornado

The deadliest tornado in U.S. history touched down at 1:00 PM on March 18, 1925. On its 219-mile (352 km) route of destruction, it passed through Missouri, Illinois, and Indiana. The twister left 695 people dead and 2,027 injured. Some 800 miners in West Frankfort, Illinois, were trapped in a mine shaft as a result of the tornado. Amazingly, they all escaped before the shaft collapsed.

One house in Indiana was pulled up from its foundation by the Tri-State Tornado and carried more than 50 feet (15 meters) from its original location.

During a tornado, some buildings might be leveled while neighboring structures are left relatively unharmed.

Flying Cows and Deadly Straw

Tornadoes are extremely unpredictable. They can completely destroy one house and leave the one next to it untouched. Tornadoes can lift cows and people and put them down hundreds of yards or meters away, sometimes safe and uninjured. In 1999, a tornado near Chickasha, Oklahoma, lifted an airplane wing from an airstrip and dropped it 70 miles (113 km) away.

Tornado Alley

Many of the worst tornadoes in the United States occur in an expanse of land known as Tornado Alley (pictured). The area experiences an average of 300 tornadoes a year. Tornado Alley is 460 miles (740 km) long and 400 miles (644 km) wide. It includes parts of Texas, Oklahoma, Kansas, and Missouri. Its exact boundaries may vary on different maps, depending on the data used.

Additional "alleys" are found elsewhere in the United States. These include Dixie Alley along the Gulf Coast and Hoosier Alley, centered in Indiana.

Tragedy in Bangladesh

Countries with poor warning systems and weak buildings have suffered the most from tornadoes. On April 26, 1989, the nation of Bangladesh experienced the deadliest tornado ever recorded. It killed 1,300 people in two cities. It also injured 12,000 and left 80,000 homeless. Within one 2.3-square-mile (6 sq km) area, every building was leveled. Between 1970 and 2010, tornadoes claimed more than 5,000 lives in this tiny, crowded country.

An average of 179 people in Bangladesh are killed by tornadoes each year—more than in any other country.

A Bangladeshi man sits among the wreckage of his home after the 1989 tornado.

Vehicles were among the damaged property in Jackson, Tennessee, as a result of the Super Tuesday tornadoes.

Super Tuesday is the day many states vote on who should run for U.S. president.

Winter Tornadoes of Super Tuesday

Tornadoes can occur at any time of year, including the winter months. On February 5 (known as "Super Tuesday") and 6, 2008, an outbreak of 86 tornadoes swept across 10 states from Indiana to Louisiana. Hardest hit were Tennessee and Kentucky, which experienced 25 tornadoes each. This two-day period holds the record for the most tornadoes in February.

Storm Chasers

To get close to tornadoes and study them, weather scientists often take to the road. At the first sign of a tornado, these adventurous experts hop in their mobile weather-tracking vehicles and race to the storm site. These mobile units are small labs on wheels. They are packed with radar devices, computers, and a variety of other tools for tracking and measuring twisters. A satellite dish on top of the vehicle helps the scientists connect to the Internet. This allows them to receive alerts and warnings for approaching tornadoes.

The most advanced tornado research project ever was named VORTEX2. It took place in 2009 and 2010. More than 80 scientists in 40

mobile units tracked and followed tornadoes around the country. Photographers took pictures and videos. Meteorologists launched weather balloons to measure temperature and wind speed in the storms. Other researchers planted small tornado pods containing measuring devices and cameras in the path of tornadoes. The pods were then picked up as tornadoes passed over them. This enabled the researchers to take pictures and record data from the center of the tornado. Scientists hope that the data from the VORTEX2 project will help improve tornado prediction, extend warning times, and save lives.

In areas where tornadoes are common, some people have special shelters underground where they can wait safely for a storm to pass.

CHAPTER 4

Means of Survival

Unlike hurricanes, which can be detected days before striking land, tornadoes often spring up with little warning. But even 15 minutes' notice can make a difference. If you're prepared ahead of time and follow some important safety tips, you can survive even the most destructive tornado. Knowing what to do when a twister strikes can mean the difference between life and death.

The word *tornado* comes from the Spanish word *tronada*, meaning "thunderstorm."

Be Prepared

If you live in a region where tornadoes occur regularly, you should be prepared in advance for the sudden appearance of a twister. You should have a plan even if you live in an area where tornadoes are less common. Know where you and your family will find shelter if a tornado comes. Be ready to turn on the radio or television and pay attention to emergency weather updates. If you have a computer, get familiar with the Web site of your local National Weather Service office.

Alerts can be sent to cell phones to warn people of a tornado nearby.

Know Your Warnings

Three kinds of tornado alerts are broadcast by the National Weather Service. A "tornado watch" means that conditions are in place for tornadoes to develop. Have your escape plan in mind and keep tuned to the TV or radio for further updates. A "tornado warning" means that a tornado has been sighted nearby. At this point, you should seek shelter. A "tornado emergency" means a serious tornado is about to strike a large populated area. You should seek the safest shelter immediately.

Civil defense sirens often accompany a tornado warning, letting the public know to take cover.

Signs in the Sky

How can you tell if a tornado is approaching when you are away from home and have no access to TV, radio, or the Internet? Just look to the sky. If you are experiencing heavy rains or hail and there is suddenly a dead calm, a tornado may be brewing. Another sign to look for is debris spinning or whirling at ground level beneath a storm cloud. Take cover. It's a tornado!

Some tornadoes are preceded by intense hail and rain.

If you have a bicycle helmet, put it on to protect your head during a tornado.

Students in Aurora, Colorado, cover their heads during a tornado warning in 2014.

Taking Shelter

If you live somewhere with a basement or a cyclone cellar, head downstairs. If neither is available, you should move to the interior part of the lowest floor. Go to an inside bedroom, bathroom, or closet. Avoid any room with windows. They could burst and send broken glass flying toward you. Crawl under the largest piece of furniture you can find. If there isn't any furniture nearby, crouch down and cover your head with your arms.

If you live in an unanchored mobile home, get out immediately. Like cars, these structures can become airborne in tornadoes.

The interior of a car is not a safe place to be during a tornado.

On the Road

If you're riding in a car when a tornado hits, the driver should park and everyone should get out immediately. Tornado winds can lift the vehicle or flip it over. And cars cannot outrace a tornado. Take shelter in the nearest building. If there are no buildings nearby, lie down in a ditch, **culvert,** or even a cave. Be sure there are no power lines nearby. Avoid highway and bridge overpasses. Winds will whip right through them.

In the Open

If you're outdoors and there are no shelters or low areas to run to, what should you do? Lie flat on the ground, with your face down. Hold your arms over your head. Tornado winds are weakest at ground level. Stay away from trees. They can be uprooted and tossed around by strong winds. One-third of all people who die in tornadoes are killed by flying objects or debris.

Even large trees can be torn from the ground and tossed around during a powerful tornado.

Tornado researchers measure the speed and size of a twister in action.

CHAPTER **5**

Tracking Tornadoes

Scientists can predict and track the thunderstorms that may produce tornadoes. However, predicting where and when the actual tornadoes will strike is difficult. To gain more accurate data about tornadoes and how they are born and die, meteorologists have developed useful tools to gather information. Their investigative research has taken them right to the source—the tornadoes themselves.

Storm spotters are specially trained in classes taught by local National Weather Service Forecast Offices.

Doppler Radar

Radar is a type of technology that uses radio waves to determine the presence and location of a storm or tornado. **Doppler radar** can also measure temperature and wind speed and direction using three-dimensional images on a screen. On Doppler radar, a developing tornado can be seen in a thunderstorm as a fishhook-shaped object called a hook echo. However, the radar tower must be very close to the storm to detect the tornado's presence.

Timeline of Tornadoes

May 7, 1840
The Great Natchez Tornado kills 317 people in Natchez and Vidalia, Mississippi.

March 18, 1925
The Tri-State Tornado leaves 695 dead and 2,027 injured in Missouri, Illinois, and Indiana.

April 3–4, 1974
In this Super Outbreak, 148 tornadoes sweep across 13 states and Ontario, Canada, in 16 hours, claiming 335 lives and injuring more than 6,000 other people.

Storm Spotters

In addition to scientific reports, the observations of everyday people play an important role in predicting tornadoes. About 290,000 volunteer storm spotters across the country look for signs of tornadoes and report them to the nearest National Weather Service Forecast Office. Data from radar and human observers is sent to the National Weather Center in Norman, Oklahoma. This center then issues tornado alerts and warnings to the public.

April 26, 1989

The Daulatpur-Saturia Tornado in Bangladesh is the deadliest ever recorded, killing 1,300 and leaving 80,000 homeless.

April 27, 2014

Fifteen people die in a tornado outbreak near Little Rock, Arkansas.

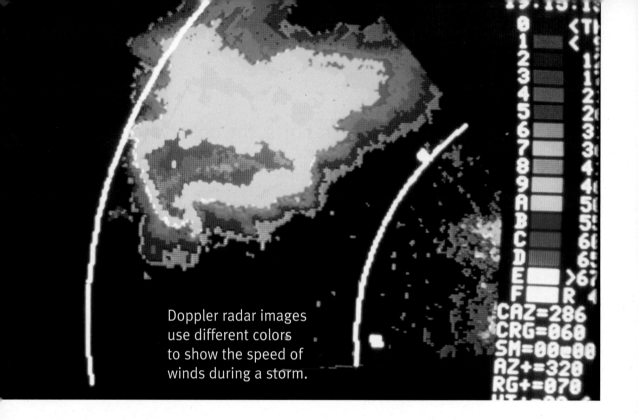

Doppler radar images use different colors to show the speed of winds during a storm.

Good News

The frequency of tornado outbreaks has been decreasing in recent decades. In the early 1970s, tornadoes occurred an average of 150 days per year. From 2000 to 2010, that number dropped to 100 days. In the first three weeks of March 2015, not a single tornado was reported anywhere in the United States, which is a very rare situation.

Bad News

At the same time, the number of days with multiple tornadoes has been growing. Over the past 10 years, 20 percent of all tornadoes in the United States took place on just three days each year. It is possible that climate change plays a role in these changes. All we know for certain is that tornadoes will continue to leave destruction in their paths. The more we learn about these fearsome events, the better we can deal with their devastating power. ★

Doppler radar technology relies on a network of weather stations that tracks the progress of storms.

Average number of tornado events that occur in the United States each year: 1,179

Average number of people killed in the United States by tornadoes each year: 60

Average economic loss from tornadoes in the U.S. each year: $1,086,575,000

Nations with the highest number of annual tornadoes: United States, Argentina, and Bangladesh

Month with the most "top 10 calendar days" for tornadoes in the U.S.: May (6 days)

Most tornadoes ever in a single outbreak in the United States: 350 on April 25–28, 2011

Did you find the truth?

(T) More tornadoes happen in the United States than anywhere else on Earth.

(F) Only hurricanes have faster, more powerful winds than tornadoes.

Resources

Books

Carson, Mary Kay. *Inside Tornadoes*. New York: Sterling, 2010.

Fradin, Judith Bloom, and Dennis Brindell Fradin. *Tornado! The Story Behind These Twisting, Turning, Spinning, and Spiraling Storms.* Washington, DC: National Geographic, 2011.

Kostigen, Thomas. *Extreme Weather: Surviving Tornadoes, Sandstorms, Hailstorms, Blizzards, Hurricanes, and More!* Washington, DC: National Geographic, 2014.

Visit this Scholastic Web site for more information on tornadoes:

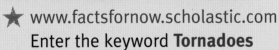 www.factsfornow.scholastic.com
Enter the keyword **Tornadoes**

Important Words

culvert (KUL-vurt) a drain or channel crossing under a road

debris (duh-BREE) pieces of something that has been broken or destroyed

diameter (dye-AM-i-tur) the length of a line passing through the center of a circular object

Doppler radar (DAHP-lur RAY-dar) a radar device that can determine the speed and direction of a moving object

meteorologist (mee-tee-uh-RAH-luh-jist) an expert in the study of Earth's atmosphere

outbreak (OUT-brake) a series of tornadoes that break out from thunderstorms at the same time

supercells (SOO-pur-selz) violent thunderstorms that sometimes give birth to tornadoes

vortex (VOR-teks) a whirling mass of air that forms a tornado

Index

Page numbers in **bold** indicate illustrations.

About the Author

Steven Otfinoski has written more than 170 books for young readers. He has written books about blizzards, volcanoes, and other natural disasters. He also teaches writing at two universities in Connecticut, where he lives with his family.

PHOTOGRAPHS ©: cover: Jim Reed/National Geographic Creative; back cover: Lissandra Melo/Shutterstock, Inc.; 3: Mike Hollingshead/age fotostock/Superstock, Inc.; 4: Eddie J. Rodriquez/Shutterstock, Inc.; 5 top: ZUMA Press, Inc/Alamy Images; 5 bottom: pedrosala/Shutterstock, Inc.; 6: Fred Stewart/AP Images; 8: ZUMA Press, Inc/Alamy Images; 9: Nam Y. Huh/AP Images; 10: Steve Pyle/AP Images; 11: Frank Anderson/AP Images; 12: Mike Hollingshead/Superstock, Inc.; 14: Robert Postma/All Canada Photos/Superstock, Inc.; 15: Designua/Shutterstock, Inc.; 16: Tony Gutierrez/AP Images; 17: John Huntington/Shutterstock, Inc.; 18: Bettmann/Corbis Images; 19: ellepistock/Shutterstock, Inc.; 20: RooM the Agency/Alamy Images; 22: Warren Price Photography/Shutterstock, Inc.; 23: AP Images; 24: Jeff Tuttle/AP Images; 26: AFP/Getty Images; 27: Christopher Berkey/AP Images; 28, 29 background: Mike Hollingshead/age fotostock/Superstock, Inc.; 28 inset: Ryan McGinnis/Alamy Images; 29 inset: Jim Reed/Science Source; 30: FEMA/Alamy Images; 32: David Mercer/AP Images; 33: Eddie J. Rodriquez/Shutterstock, Inc.; 34: dpa picture alliance archive/Alamy Images; 35: Joe Amon/Getty Images; 36: Julie Dermansky/Science Source; 37: VisionsofAmerica/Joe Sohm/Getty Images; 38: Howard Bluestein/Science Source; 40: Frank Anderson/AP Images; 41: AFP/Getty Images; 42: Science Source; 43: pedrosala/Shutterstock, Inc.; 44: Mike Hollingshead/age fotostock/Superstock, Inc.

Map by Design Lab